Come into My Garden

JANELLE M. ANDERSON

Many blessings!
Janelle Anderson
4/13/18

ISBN:1981467750
ISBN-13: 978-1981467754

DEDICATION

To my mom, Betty LeDoux, a most beautiful, gentle soul
Who so lovingly led me into the arms of Love
When I was entirely lost and broken;
And introduced me to incomprehensible Peace
So that I could come home again.

She now dances in heaven with Jesus,
her garden in full bloom.

CONTENTS

FOREWORD

Come into My Garden by Janelle Anderson will take you places you have only dreamed of. Your heart will be touched and melted by the power and intimacy of the words spoken by Jesus in these twenty devotionals. You will experience healing of your own heart as you bask in the rays of Christ's healing touch upon Janelle's heart. The visions are powerful. His love is intense and His wisdom is penetrating.

The Bible is clear that in the last days God will pour out His spirit, and we will prophecy and see visions (Acts 2:17). Well, this book is a fulfillment of that promise. In an age hungry for spiritual reality, this book provides it. It is exciting to see that the four keys to hearing God's voice are so wonderfully transferable. I shared them with Janelle, and in her first devotional she shares them with you. Then Janelle provides you twenty examples of them in action. May you too learn to hear God's voice and see His visions, and receive the life, love and power of Almighty God.

Dr. Mark Virkler
Communion with God Ministries
Christian Leadership University

JANELLE M. ANDERSON

INTRODUCTION:
HOW TO HEAR GOD'S VOICE

Over a decade ago, I enrolled in a course called *"How to Hear God's Voice"* through Christian Leadership University and Communion with God Ministries. That course absolutely revolutionized not only my quiet times with the Lord, but also impacted my level of intimacy with God in every part of my life. This book is a direct result of what I learned in that course. It is a collection of journal entries over the years – a record of incredible conversations with Jesus. In these prayer times, I used the following 4 keys taught by Dr. Mark Virkler.

How to Hear God's Voice by Dr. Mark Virkler

Habakkuk said, "I will stand on my guard post..." (Hab. 2:1). **The first key to hearing God's voice is to go to a quiet place and still our own thoughts and emotions.** Psalm 46:10 encourages us to be still, let go, cease striving, and know that He is God. In Psalm 37:7 we are called to "be still before the Lord and wait patiently for Him." There is a deep inner knowing in our spirits that each of us can experience when we quiet our flesh and our minds. Practicing the art of biblical meditation helps silence the outer noise and distractions clamoring for our attention.

"I will keep watch to see," said the prophet. To receive the pure word of God, it is very important that my heart be properly focused as I become still, because my focus is the source of the intuitive flow. If I fix my eyes upon Jesus (Heb. 12:2), the intuitive flow comes from Jesus. But if I fix my gaze upon some desire of my heart, the intuitive flow comes out of that desire. To have a pure flow I must become still and carefully fix my eyes upon Jesus. Quietly worshiping the King and receiving out of the stillness that follows quite easily accomplishes this.

3

So, the second key to hearing God's voice: As you pray, fix the eyes of your heart upon Jesus, seeing in the Spirit the dreams and visions of Almighty God. Habakkuk was actually looking for vision as he prayed. He opened the eyes of his heart and looked into the spirit world to see what God wanted to show him. God has always spoken through dreams and visions, and He specifically said that they would come to those upon whom the Holy Spirit is poured out (Acts 2:1-4, 17).

In order to see, we must look. Daniel saw a vision in his mind and said, "I was looking...I kept looking...I kept looking" (Dan. 7:2, 9, 13). As I pray, I look for Jesus, and I watch as He speaks to me, doing and saying the things that are on His heart. Many Christians will find that if they will only look, they will see. Jesus is Emmanuel, God with us (Matt. 1:23). It is as simple as that. You can see Christ present with you because Christ *is* present with you. **In fact, the vision may come so easily that you will be tempted to reject it, thinking that it is just you.** But if you persist in recording these visions, your doubt will soon be overcome by faith as you recognize that the content of them could only be birthed in Almighty God.

Jesus demonstrated the ability of living out of constant contact with God, declaring that He did nothing on His own initiative, but only what He saw the Father doing, and heard the Father saying (Jn. 5:19,20,30). What an incredible way to live!

Is it possible for us to live out of divine initiative as Jesus did? Yes! We must simply fix our eyes upon Jesus. The veil has been torn, giving access into the immediate presence of God, and He calls us to draw near (Lk. 23:45; Heb. 10:19-22). "I pray that the eyes of your heart will be enlightened...."

I had previously listened for an inner audible voice, and God does speak that way at times. However, I have found that usually,

God's voice comes as spontaneous thoughts, visions, feelings, or impressions.

For example, haven't you been driving down the road and had a thought come to you to pray for a certain person? Didn't you believe it was God telling you to pray? What did God's voice sound like? Was it an audible voice, or was it a spontaneous thought that lit upon your mind?

Experience indicates that we perceive spirit-level communication as **spontaneous thoughts, impressions and visions,** and Scripture confirms this in many ways. For example, one definition of *paga*, a Hebrew word for intercession, is "a chance encounter or an accidental intersecting." When God lays people on our hearts, He does it through *paga*, a chance-encounter thought "accidentally" intersecting our minds.

So, the third key to hearing God's voice is recognizing that God's voice in your heart often sounds like a flow of spontaneous thoughts. Therefore, when I want to hear from God, I tune to chance-encounter or spontaneous thoughts.

Finally, God told Habakkuk to record the vision (Hab. 2:2). This was not an isolated command. The Scriptures record many examples of individual's prayers and God's replies, such as the Psalms, many of the prophets, and Revelation. I have found that obeying this final principle amplified my confidence in my ability to hear God's voice so that I could finally make living out of His initiatives a way of life. **The fourth key, two-way journaling or the writing out of your prayers and God's answers, brings great freedom in hearing God's voice.**

The four simple keys that the Lord showed me from Habakkuk have been used by people of all ages, from four to a hundred and four, from every continent, culture and denomination, to break through into intimate two-way conversations with their loving Father and dearest Friend. Omitting any one of the keys will prevent you from receiving all He wants to say to you. The order of the keys is not important, just that you *use them all*. Embracing all four, by faith, can change your life. **Simply quiet yourself down, tune to spontaneity, look for vision, and journal. He is waiting to meet you there.**

You will be amazed when you journal! Doubt may hinder you at first, but throw it off, reminding yourself that it is a biblical concept, and that God is present, speaking to His children. Relax. When we cease our labors and enter His rest, God is free to flow (Heb. 4:10).

Why not try it for yourself, right now? Sit back comfortably, take out your pen and paper, and smile. Turn your attention toward the Lord in praise and worship, seeking His face. Many people have found the music and visionary prayer called "A Stroll Along the Sea of Galilee" helpful in getting them started. You can listen to it and download it free at www.CWGMinistries.org/Galilee.

After you write your question to Him, become still, fixing your gaze on Jesus. You will suddenly have a very good thought. Don't doubt it; simply write it down. Later, as you read your journaling, you, too, will be blessed to discover that you are indeed dialoguing with God. If you wonder if it is really the Lord speaking to you, share it with your spouse or a friend. Their input will encourage your faith and strengthen your commitment to spend time getting to know the Lover of your soul more intimately than you ever dreamed possible.

Is It *Really* God?

Five ways to be sure what you're hearing is from Him:

1) Test the Origin (1 Jn. 4:1)

Thoughts from our own minds are progressive, with one thought leading to the next, however tangentially. Thoughts from the spirit world are spontaneous. The Hebrew word for true prophecy is *naba,* which literally means to bubble up, whereas false prophecy is *ziyd* meaning to boil up. True words from the Lord will bubble up from our innermost being; we don't need to cook them up ourselves.

2) Compare It to Biblical Principles

God will never say something to you personally which is contrary to His universal revelation as expressed in the Scriptures. If the Bible clearly states that something is a sin, no amount of journaling can make it right. Much of what you journal about will not be specifically addressed in the Bible, however, so an understanding of biblical principles is also needed.

3) Compare It to the Names and Character of God as Revealed in the Bible

Anything God says to you will be in harmony with His essential nature. Journaling will help you get to *know* God personally but knowing what the Bible says *about* Him will help you discern what words are from Him. Make sure the tenor of your journaling lines up with the character of God as described in the names of the Father, Son and Holy Spirit.

4) Test the Fruit (Matt. 7:15-20)

What effect does what you are hearing have on your soul and your spirit? Words from the Lord will quicken your faith and increase your love, peace and joy. They will stimulate a sense of humility within you as you become more aware of Who God is and who you are. On the other hand, any words you receive which cause you to fear or doubt, which bring you into confusion or anxiety, or which stroke your ego (especially if you hear something that is "just for you alone – no one else is worthy") must be immediately rebuked and rejected as lies of the enemy.

5) Share It with Your Spiritual Counselors (Prov. 11:14)

We are members of a Body! A cord of three strands is not easily broken and God's intention has always been for us to grow together. Nothing will increase your faith in your ability to hear from God like having it confirmed by two or three other people! Share it with your spouse, your parents, your friends, your elder, your group leader, even your grown children can be your sounding board. They don't need to be perfect or super-spiritual; they just need to love you, be committed to being available to you, have a solid biblical orientation, and most importantly, they must also willingly and easily receive counsel. Avoid the authoritarian who insists that because of their standing in the church or with God, they no longer need to listen to others. Find two or three people and let them confirm that you are hearing from God!

The book *4 Keys to Hearing God's Voice* is available at www.CWGMinistries.org.
©CWG Ministries, Mark and Patti Virkler. Used with Permission.

How to Use this Book:

As you read this book (part devotional, part journal, and part Bible study), you will see the 4 keys in use as described above by Dr. Virkler. Each chapter begins with a section called **"The Vision."** This is a description of what I "saw" in my mind as I opened the eyes of my heart to the Lord, after quieting myself down. The vision is followed by what I heard the Lord speak to my heart as I tuned to the flow of those spontaneous thoughts and recorded them as they came to me.

Following each entry is a section called **"Going Deeper."** This is where I verified what I heard by going to scripture. This part is a mini-Bible study as I delve deeper into the scripture that my journal entry relates to.

Next, you will find a section called **"Your Turn."** This is an invitation for you to try it for yourself. There is space for you to journal right here in this book or you can use a separate journal. Quiet yourself before the Lord, open the eyes of your heart, tune to the spontaneous voice of God and start writing!

A Word of Caution: When you journal for yourself, please use the scriptures included in each chapter as your source and when you tune to flow, **ask God what He wants to speak to you from those verses**. Please do not use my visions and journal entries as your source. Those are the things He spoke to me and as I certainly hope they inspire, comfort and encourage you, they are not Scripture. God has different things He wants to speak to you. Let your journaling flow from having your eyes fixed on Jesus alone!

There are also additional Scripture verses at the end of each chapter for further study and meditation.

This book is designed to be a journey, not a race. I strongly recommend that you take much time with each chapter. You can easily spend two to three days on each one if you journal on one Scripture verse per day. Although there are 20 devotionals, this could be a 60-90 day prayer journal. Sit with each one and allow the Holy Spirit to unpack the treasures hidden there for you. Linger with Jesus there in the secret garden and breathe in the sweetness of His presence. Let Him speak kindly to your heart and hold you close to His heart.

You will be transformed and changed from glory to glory as you draw closer to the heart of God and begin to hear His voice more and more clearly for yourself. May you be filled with the joy and peace that comes from walking in close communion and intimacy with Jesus every day.

All Scripture verses are cited from the New American Standard Bible.

1 - HOW DO YOU SEE ME, LORD?

I was sitting outside. I felt impressed to tune in to the nature around me. I heard the varied bird songs high up in the trees, felt the gentle breeze on my face, breathed in the sweet aromas of the grass and flowers, and watched as a graceful deer stood quietly watching me from the far side of the yard.

I heard one word over and over being whispered to my heart:

Gentleness

He sees me like:

A gentle blowing breeze
Sweet songs of the birds
Gracefulness of the deer

You are a song to my heart,
A breath of fresh air kissing my face.
The sweet aromas of flowers; such sweet delight
Refreshment to my heart.
You are a sip of sweet wine,
The beauty of a golden sunset,
A fragrant rose to me.
So exquisite,
So pleasing,
So delightful,
Are you to Me, My love.

2 - THE LOCKED GARDEN

"A garden locked is my sister, my bride. A rock garden locked, a spring sealed up. Your shoots are an orchard of pomegranates with choice fruits, henna with nard plants. Nard and saffron, calamus and cinnamon, with all the trees of frankincense, myrrh and aloes, along with all the finest spices. You are a garden spring, a well of fresh water and streams flowing from Lebanon. Awake, O north wind, and come, wind of the south; make my garden breathe out fragrance, let its spices be wafted abroad. May my beloved come into his garden and eat its choice fruits!" **Song of Solomon 4:12-16**

The Vision:

I see a walled garden. It is FULL of lush plants and trees, vines are growing up all the walls and spilling over the wall to the outside. I see Jesus walking along the outside of the wall, standing up on tiptoe to peek over the wall, looking for the opening into the garden. He finds the gate and it is unlocked and ajar. His face lights up with a huge smile and He throws His head back and laughs joyfully. Then He opens the gate and walks into the garden. He is obviously so excited to be in this garden. He looks around with pleasure at all the lushness, the fruits, the beauty and breathes in the fragrances.

Then He takes some fruit from a vine on the wall and takes a bite. He throws His head back, opens up His arms and shouts with joy! He looks around Him like He is taking inventory of this garden. As I look deeper into the vision, I notice that only the area near the gate is cleared. The ground is clear, the plants trimmed and rich with fruit. The paths going into the garden don't go very far, however. They go out in all directions for a short distance, and then are stopped by thick undergrowth and thorns cover the plants. Beyond this point, the plants all seem to be covered by something. I noticed a spring bubbling up from the ground in several places and there is water trickling along the ground.

I see the Lord taking out some pruning shears and other tools and start to work in one of the overgrown areas.

What are You saying to me, Lord?

I am overjoyed that you have opened up your garden (inner self, soul) to Me and I can come in and eat of the fruit of your life. Your fruit is sweet to my taste and your fragrances delight Me beyond measure. You are My garden of delights and I want all of you for myself. The springs of Life are flowing in you and watering your soul, bringing healing and refreshing and life to areas that have been neglected and shrouded in darkness. We are working together to open up more pathways for My life to grow in you so that you may bear much more fruit.

Don't be afraid to go into the areas I am pruning and clearing. Open up more to Me and allow Me complete access to those areas in your heart that have been hidden for many years.

Going Deeper:

This vision marked the beginning of my journey to true freedom. The name of this book comes from this vision because it was such a turning point in my life. You see, I had been hiding many things from my past in deep places in my heart for decades. I thought my painful past was safely stowed away never again to see the light of day – never to be spoken of or even thought about. After all, I had become a Christian and had asked for forgiveness for my sins, hadn't I? Wasn't it all "under the blood"?

While that was all certainly true, what I didn't realize until the day I saw this vision in prayer was that even though my sins were completely forgiven and washed away, there was still work to be done. I had been living my life from the edge, the outer part, of my heart for 35 years. When people would ask about my testimony, I only told parts of it. I couldn't tell all of it – what would they think? My heart was still covered in shame and that shame held me back from true freedom and transparency.

When I saw this vision, I had been crying out to the Lord because I felt like there was something blocking me from going deeper into His presence, holding me back from true intimacy with Him and with others. I was always hiding a part of me, though mostly I was unaware of it. He showed me this vision so that I would see that I had a choice. My true freedom would come only when I chose to allow Him to go deeper into my heart, into my past, into the dark areas shrouded in shame, not because He wanted to hurt me or bring me pain, but so that He could cleanse my heart completely, clear away all the debris and pain and make a way for more fruit to grow. But, it was clearly up to me.

He was waiting for my permission to go there.

I did not say yes for another whole year!

Why? In one word – FEAR.

Fear of feeling the pain again, looking at what I had done and what had been done to me, and the fear of others knowing. I knew I had to have help going there which meant someone else would hear my story.

But the pain of not experiencing the intimacy with the Father that I longed for, thirsted and hungered for, was greater and I finally said YES!

And you know the amazing part of it? The things I was so afraid of never even happened! He cut to the root of it all in one fell swoop and all the shame fell away. There was no pain, only grieving, but it was a good cleansing type of grief. Deep cleansing took place and I knew I was finally, truly free.

More healing came over time when I was able to tell my story to people without shame, without fear, but instead with love and gratitude that God had redeemed me and restored me. It was my story and I was finally able to own it. Owning my story without shame has empowered other women to open up the garden of their hearts and receive the cleansing power of God's unconditional love and forgiveness for them, too. My story is a part of me, a part of my life, because I lived it and it has had an impact on who I am. I am stronger and more compassionate because of what I have lived through. It is my story, but it is no longer dark or shameful. It is redeemed in His love because I am no longer defined by what happened to me or by what I have done. My identity is established by the Lord. My identity is that I am God's daughter and His beloved one. That's who I've always been.

Beloved, He truly delights in you – in every part of you! He sees your true beauty underneath all the pain, hurt and shame. He's not looking at your sins or your failures. He's looking at your true heart – your true soul and spirit – made in His image and likeness – and that beauty brings Him immeasurable pleasure and delight! He only wants to cleanse you and bring out your beauty so you can shine with pure light and so that you can walk in freedom.

Shame shrouds our hearts and causes us to want to hide. The love of Jesus cuts it away and causes us to shine from our true selves. Invite Him into your garden today and give him access to every part of your heart. Say yes – and be free!

For further reading and meditation:

Isaiah 51:3
Isaiah 54:4-8

Your Turn: Ask Him to speak to you from this verse. What is He saying to you about the garden of your heart? Then, record what He speaks to you below or in your journal.

3 - COME AWAY WITH ME

"Arise, my darling, my beautiful one, and come along! O, my dove, in the clefts of the rock, in the secret place of the steep pathway, let me see your form, let me hear your voice; for your voice is sweet, and your form is lovely." **Song of Solomon 2:13-14**

The Vision:

I see a curtain before me. Where the opening is, the curtain is moving, softly fluttering, opening a bit, enticing me to draw near. I hear the most beautiful music playing somewhere behind the curtain, the heart-melting melody draws me like a magnet. This is clearly an invitation, mysterious and irresistible at the same time.

As I move closer and closer, I feel my whole being carried toward this place as if I were in a stream flowing with the current. There's nothing I want more than to step inside that curtain. I pull back the curtain and go inside.

Immediately, I am enveloped by the most intense sense of pleasure and delight – beyond anything I have ever experienced or could even imagine! All my senses are alive and electrified with joy! The music I heard earlier now fills my entire being, every cell in my body is a part of the melody. It's like the music is coming from me, but it is also filling everything else.

I look around and my eyes can hardly bear to gaze upon the beauty before me. The most vibrant colors everywhere, like rainbows splashing out from the lushest plants and trees, the sky, the grass, everything. I see a path lined with rainbows and as I begin to walk along the path, my feet are massaged and soothed by the ground itself. It seems to be alive and forms to my feet, supporting and wrapping around them like the most perfect shoes ever! The path seems to be bearing my weight up under it and kind of moving me along.

Soon I arrive at a clearing where the trees form a canopy over the area, like a private little alcove. I see Jesus sitting there, waiting for me with the most exquisite smile, His eyes of love rest on my face and fill me with such love. Instantly, I know I belong here.

Jesus motions for me to sit next to Him and I see that there is a feast set before us. As I settle into the most comfortable seat I've ever known, I realize I am in the Secret Place. I turn to look into His face and immediately I am lost in those eyes of love.

What are You saying to me, Lord?

I want you to come after Me, to run after Me, with all your heart, with all your soul, with all your might, and with all your power. Make a holy place for Me to rest and for My Spirit to alight, for I long to be with you and for you to be with Me. It is the delight and pleasure of My heart to be with you in this holy place you create with your worship.

A holy place is a place set apart just for Me, where you focus all your attention and all your energy and all your passion only on Me, your Lover and your Friend. I love that holy, secret place of communion when your heart is set only on Me – no distractions, no competition, no person, project or task, no trial, idea or image vying for your time and attention. I love that place of intimacy with you. **This is what I created you for!** This is where I can pour My love and My life into you in unhindered extravagance and you become filled to overflowing, satisfied to the depths of your being. You were made for love, for My love. This is what you are longing and searching for!

No striving or self-determination will transport you to this place. You cannot get here by your own might and strength. You cannot force your way into this place. No, it is only when you come before Me humbly and surrendered; when you gently unveil your heart before Me in faith and trust, your entire being yielded to Me, every place in your heart open to Me - no hiding, no excuses, no resisting.

This is how you enter the secret place of My presence.

This is a place of sweet surrender where you invite Me into the garden of your soul and allow Me to have My way in you. That is when the beauty I have created in you begins to be unveiled as My glory shines through you. This is where your soul finds rest and walks in peace even in the midst of the life's storms. When you live out of the secret, holy place, it does not matter what the outer circumstances are, you will scarcely notice them. They will not really matter. Your eyes, your heart, your mind, your soul will be fixed on Me alone. I will live through you – My life and power will flow through you.

Come away with Me, My beloved!

Going Deeper:

Jesus delights in being with us in the secret place. This is astounding! The language in these verses is breathtaking! We need to understand the deeper meaning of the words. The word "arise" has many applications, but basically it means to stand up and also **to become powerful and to come on the scene.**

Think about what happens when you spend time in the secret place with the Lord. You become empowered, don't you? You are awakened from your slumber and suddenly find that you have "come on the scene." You are present and awake, alive to the destiny you are called to fulfill. Another meaning of the word is to be fulfilled! He's calling us to arise, stand up, come onto the scene of our lives and become powerful with His love pouring into us. He's calling us to be fulfilled in Him and in those things He has purposed for us to do and to be.

Then there is the last part of verse 14: "let me see your form, let me hear your voice; for your voice is sweet and your form is lovely." The word "see" is not merely a quick glance here. It means "to give attention to" and "to gaze at." It also means to look upon one another! What intimacy! He gives His attention to us and

19

spends time gazing at us.

And He longs for us to also gaze at Him in face to face communion with Him! What wonder!

When He says, "let me hear," He is saying, "I want to listen with intense attention to all the things on your heart." Wow! He is deeply invested in you! You have His undivided attention!

And finally, look at the word "voice". It means not only your voice, but the *sound of your voice.* You have a unique sound that is so sweet to His ears! No one else has your sound and no one else has your appearance or form! You are beautiful to His eyes and the sound of your voice is sweet to His ears!

Does this understanding of the intensity of the Lord's desire for you help you to see how powerful and exciting your quiet times can be? Does it stir in your soul a longing to leave everything behind and run into His presence?

He finds our voice and appearance beautiful. He longs to hear our voice and see our face. His desire is for us to come away with Him, away from the distractions of our lives and the noise of this world. Can you hear the longing in His heart for you to be alone with Him, to be totally enthralled with His love having your eyes fixed solely on Him?

Somewhere deep inside, I think we all long for this place of rest and being hidden away in the secret place of His presence. As a young girl, one of my favorite places in the whole world was a wooded area near my home. To me, it was the "enchanted forest" and when I was there, I felt like I was transported to another world where I could be a princess waiting for her prince, ready to embark on wonderful adventures together.

The truth is, we are being called to come away with our Prince and not just in our imagination. This is real and it is available to us every single day! And the best part is, we don't have to buy anything, go anywhere, become someone we are not, go through a set of steps or rituals, or be anyone other than just who we are right now.

He is waiting always, peering through the lattice, reaching through the doorway to touch our hungry hearts, waiting by the well, hoping we will come. He longs for us to come to Him, just as we are! As soon as we turn our heart His way, He is there to carry us away to the mountain of spices with Him. All we need to do is quiet our souls, be still, turn our attention full on Him and say, "Jesus, take me away!"

For further reading and meditation:

Psalm 91:1-4
Psalm 27:4-5
Matthew 11:28-30

Your Turn: Ask the Lord what He wants to say to you about coming into the secret place. Next, record below or in your journal what He speaks to you.

4 - FOREVER IS IN YOUR HEART

"Jesus said to them, 'I am the bread of life; he who comes to Me shall not hunger, and he who believes in Me shall never thirst.'"
John 6:35

The Vision:

I'm standing on a sandy hill overlooking the ocean. All up and down the beach, there is a long table stretching endlessly in both directions, as far as the eye can see. There is no end to this table. It is filled with food and drink, wholesome, nutritious fruits and vegetables, meats and fish, nuts, seeds, figs, and dates. People are seated at the table, feasting, laughing, conversing, and enjoying each other. Every person has a glass of wine and they toast each other often. With all of this food and drink laid out on the table, what stands out the most is the bread.

The bread is like one long endless loaf stretching the length of this endless table and as people break off pieces of it, the hole where they tore the piece fills back in and it's like nothing was taken at all. The bread itself is endless. When the people eat the bread, there is a light that glows out from their heart and they seem to tingle with delight and joy. This bread seems to be giving them life itself.

As I observe this joyous feast, I slowly realize that every time someone beaks off a piece of the bread, they always hand it to someone else. No one ever takes bread for themselves. It is always given away. The joy from this single act is palpable. I can actually feel it emanating from the people as they share the bread with one another.

What are You saying to me, Lord?

Forever is in your heart. Everyone longs for it and looks for it and yet it is right there in your heart. You were created for eternity, to live with me forever. No soul is satisfied until it meets me there in the eternal place of the heart. This is what I was trying to tell them that day by the sea when I told them about the Bread of Heaven that satisfies. The hungry soul will be satisfied with me, the Bread of Heaven.

Come and eat, come and drink and be satisfied! There is nothing greater you will ever find in this world. It is the greatest news ever told that the Bread of Heaven has come and all can freely eat of it. All of creation knows this, even the bird singing outside your window this morning. All creation groans because it waits for the fullness of this truth to be realized by men. The enemy has blinded so many and yet they hunger so!

You have the bread of heaven in your soul. Feed on it and allow it to transform you and make you like Me. Hold it out to this hungry world and let them see it and taste it. I am hungry, too. I am hungry for all the lost souls to find true peace, to find true love, to find the bread that satisfies. I am hungry for them to come to Me.

As I said, "He who comes to Me will never go hungry, and he who believes in Me will never be thirsty." All they need to do is come and believe and I will fill them. All you need to do is hold out the Bread to them. Let them see it and pray for their eyes to be opened. That's all I am asking of you.

I asked: How do I hold out the bread to them, Jesus?

You do it when you treat others with kindness and compassion and when you care about them. When you smile at others and ask about their day and take the time to listen to their hearts. Imagine that you are worshiping me in song when you talk to others and offer it up to me. You will be amazed at what happens. The exchange will become a song of worship to Me!

Just remember that it is always all about Me. I Am the Bread of Life and I Am the Answer to every question and the Solution to every problem of the human race. I came that they may have Life and have it more abundantly. There is nothing that you can offer others in and of yourself. You can only offer ME!

I am their only hope. So worship Me as you interact with people and you will be holding out to them this Bread of Heaven.

Going Deeper:

This verse appears right in the middle of a very controversial conversation Jesus had with His followers. By the end of it, many people left Him because they could not comprehend what He was saying. They thought He was being literal when He said in verse 53, "Truly, truly, I say to you, unless you eat the flesh of the Son of Man and drink His blood, you have no life in yourselves."

Of course, He was not declaring that they should become cannibals. In verse 63 He explains that the words He has spoken are spirit and life. Even so, what Jesus said in this passage still causes people to walk away from eternal life. Why?

Because what He declared was total union with Him, not holding anything back, being all in! When you eat and drink something, you consume it and it becomes a part of your being – total unity. There is no separation. It literally becomes a part of your body, down to the cellular level. And it gives life to you – food and drink are the sustenance of life. You cannot continue being without consuming food and drink, right?

Jesus claimed that He is THE Bread of Life and that when we consume Him, He becomes a part of our very being – and we will live forever as a result!

For further reading and meditation:

John 6:35-65
John 3:10-16

Your Turn: Ask the Lord what He wants to say to you about the Bread of Life. Record below or in your journal what He speaks to you.

5 – CLOTHED IN GLORY

"I will rejoice greatly in the Lord, My soul will exult in my God; for He has clothed me with garments of salvation, He has wrapped me with a robe of righteousness, as a bridegroom decks himself with a garland, and as a bride adorns herself with her jewels."
Isaiah 61:10

The Vision:

I'm at a party, it seems. I'm walking from room to room in this house and every room is filled with people standing in small groups, talking and laughing and having a great time. But I'm like a ghost. I'm moving through the crowd, silently and invisibly. No one sees me or talks to me. It's like I'm there, but I'm not.

I notice a door is open to a room. Out of curiosity, I go inside and look around. Then I realize I'm standing in a closet, a huge closet filled with clothes hanging all around the room, on all four sides. The strange thing is that all of the clothes in this room are just rags. They are worn out, torn, frayed, dirty clothes. There is a distinct odor coming from these clothes, a stench really, and it makes me want to gag. I want to get out of there, but when I turn to go, I find I'm standing in front of a full-length mirror.

When I catch sight of my reflection in the mirror, I gasp in horror. I see that I am dressed in rags, too, just like the clothes in this closet! I stand there in shock and disbelief, frozen there in that spot, not knowing what to do.

Then a door to my right opens up and light streams out bathing me in its warmth. I am being called into this light. As I step in, I see the most glorious dress hanging in front of me. It is covered in jewels and shimmers with exquisite beauty. There is a stunningly beautiful crown and golden shoes on a table nearby.

With a dawning realization, I know that this dress is meant for me.

What are You saying to me, Lord?

Come out of the shadows, step into the light. Shine bright for I have clothed you in my glory and you are beautiful. If you stay in the shadow of who you are and all I have created you to be, you will never shine your brilliance into all the places where I have ordained you to have a great impact.

It's only when you come out of the shadows of timidity, shame and fear of inadequacy and step into the place perfectly fitted for you alone that your voice will resound and reverberate. My presence in you will change the atmosphere. It's time to come out with joy! It's time to rejoice and dance because I have adorned you in my exquisite beauty as I shine through you!

Going Deeper:

I didn't realize I was wearing the wrong clothes – not for a long time. The robe of shame I wrapped myself in did not make me very joyful. Oh, I could be outwardly joyful and happy for periods of time, but deep inside mostly I was hiding under my cloak of shame and fear. But I didn't know it was there. It seemed normal – like this was the normal Christian life. It was normal to go through the motions and check all the boxes, like prayer, Bible study, worship, go to church, go to work, clean house, cook dinner, spend time with family, and so on.

But then I began to deeply hunger for more, to thirst for the living water to be stirred up in my spirit and poured out in abundance, to be continually filled by this incredible Holy Spirit – that deep river inside. That's when I started to wake up.

And when I started to wake up, becoming aware of who I am and who I was created to be, I began to really SEE that *He has wrapped me* in His beautiful garments and *He has adorned me* with His brilliant jewels. This was HIS doing! So, there is absolutely no longer any reason to continue wearing that cloak of shame – It is my CHOICE to throw it off and to REJOICE in my true identity as a daughter of God: brilliant, beautiful, adorned - cherished, valued, and loved.

What clothes are you wearing? Don't miss the part where it says that HE has already clothed you in garments of salvation and HE has already wrapped you in a robe of righteousness! But we so often cover up those beautiful garments with cloaks of shame and fear and we no longer can see our true identity.

What is your true identity? Let's look more closely at the fabric of our spiritual wardrobe, shall we?

He has *clothed me with garments of salvation*:

The word "clothed" literally means to be **fully clothed** or **wrapped around with**. The word "garments" means **a covering,** and the word "salvation" here is the Hebrew word *"yesha"* meaning **liberty, deliverance, freedom, welfare, and prosperity!** This means you are fully covered and wrapped in liberty, deliverance, freedom, welfare and prosperity!

He has *wrapped me with a robe of righteousness:*

The word "wrapped" means **to cover**. The word for "robe" was used to describe a long garment worn by David's daughters (the King's daughters) and it was also the word used for a garment worn by the high priest, speaking of attributes. The root word also means **covering**. What are the attributes this robe speaks of? It's a robe of **righteousness** – an attribute of God. It means to **be just and right in conduct and character.** This is what you are covered in!

As a bridegroom decks himself with a garland and a bride adorns herself with her jewels:

You are totally decked out! The garland here speaks of your **place as a priest and minister** and the jewels speak of **preparation** – having all the tools you need to accomplish, complete, and finish what you are called to do!

So rejoice! Put on your true identity in Christ, throw off your rags of shame and inadequacy, and shine in your garments of salvation. You are the beautiful Bride! Come out of hiding, step into the Light, and shine forth!

For further reading and meditation:

    Isaiah 49:1-3
    Isaiah 52:1-2
    Ephesians 2:10
    Ephesians 4:22-25
    Colossians 3:10-17

Your Turn: Ask the Lord to give you full revelation of your identity in Him! Then record below or in your journal what He speaks to you.

6 - BE IN THE SPIRIT

"I was in the Spirit on the Lord's day, and I heard behind me a loud voice like the sound of a trumpet." **Revelation 1:10**

The Vision:

I stand overlooking a massive waterfall, like Niagara Falls, overwhelmed by the sheer power and force of the falls. The sound thunders in my ears and I feel the spray of the water on my face. It is beautiful and terrifying at the same time. Two angelic beings are on either side of me and are lifting me up and carrying me over the huge chasm created by the falls and the river far below. We are flying! The sense of freedom is exhilarating and thrilling! I know that I am completely safe, but I am also aware that I am not in control in any way. This is happening with absolutely no effort on my part. It is glorious! The angels set me down on the opposite shore from where I had been standing.

What are You saying to me, Lord?

The only way to step into the Spirit is to give up all self-effort and control. You cannot step into the things of the Spirit by your own efforts. It is not by might, nor by power, but by My Spirit only that this is done. Surrender and yield yourself to My Spirit and yield completely to Me. I will carry you over to another dimension in the Spirit, to a place you cannot even imagine now, where you will see and hear so clearly and walk in power and authority that comes only from Me. It is a very different place to walk than where you have been and where you are now. That's why there is such a wide chasm between the two shores. You cannot cross over without My Spirit.

Your spirit must always be centered on Me. As John was "in the Spirit" when he received the Revelation, you must have your spirit eyes turned toward Me every day and in every circumstance. It is not by self-effort that this is done, but by yielding and turning to Me. It is a lifestyle, a daily focus, a mindset, a longing, a hungering and thirsting for the things of God and for the heart of God. Turn away from the world's ways and keep your eyes and ears focused on Me and My Spirit will teach you and shine revelation light upon you. Immerse yourself in My Word and seek Me first. My presence must be your treasure and your desire above all other things.

Step into the Spirit, step in all the way and be filled, be completed and saturated with My life. Be completely Mine. You are My beloved, My love, My joy and desire. I long to fill you completely with Myself. It is only then that you will be satisfied and whole.

Going Deeper:

What would be possible for us to hear and see and experience if we were "in the Spirit" like John? He heard a loud voice like the sound of a trumpet and then received instructions to write what he saw and send it to the churches. We know the result of this experience for John was the book of Revelation and that is a vision and assignment that we will not have because the Bible is already written. But, how many assignments and revelations do we miss daily because we are not in the Spirit? This is what I saw and heard one day as I was in prayer, listening and opening my spirit up to hear the voice "behind me."

The Greek word used for "hear" in Revelation 1:10 is *"akouo"* and it means to understand, consider, and perceive the sense of what is being said. This is a tuning in and intensely giving attention to what you are hearing. It is not a casual, surface type of listening. This type of hearing goes to the depth of understanding.

John heard behind him "a loud voice like the sound of a trumpet." The root meaning of the word for "voice" is **to bring forth with the idea of disclosure.** God had something He wanted to bring forth and disclose to us through John. Jesus called us His friends and said that He would tell us things to come, didn't He?

How do you know for sure that you are hearing the Holy Spirit speaking to you?

It comes with practice, but it is also grounded in the unshakable faith that God does still speak to His children and that we DO hear His voice.

Then, we step into the Spirit – and listen.

For further reading and meditation:

John 10:14, 27
1 Corinthians 2:9-11
1 Corinthians 3:16
Ephesians 5:18-21

Your Turn: Ask the Lord to speak to you today – And then listen. Record below or in your journal what you hear Him say.

7 - FACE THE WIND

"For He spoke and raised up a stormy wind, which lifted up the waves of the sea. They rose up to the heavens, they went down to the depths; their souls melted away in their misery. They reeled and staggered like a drunken man, and were at their wits end. Then they cried to the Lord in their trouble, and He brought them out of their distresses. He caused the storm to be still, so that the waves of the sea were hushed." **Psalm 107:25-29**

The Vision:

I stood on the edge of a great cliff when the wind began to blow. It grew in intensity and speed until I thought that I would literally be blown away. I longed to run and hide from this wind, but my feet seemed rooted to the ground. All I could do was stand and face the wind.

What are You saying to me, Lord?

Face the wind. Don't be afraid of the wind, even when it brings adversity into your life. I am standing with you as you face the winds of change and the winds of difficulties. I am at your right hand, holding you. The wind often brings something new and refreshing. It clears away the clutter and chaff in your life and brings a clean, fresh new perspective. Even when it is blowing hard, set your face into it and let it blow over you.

The wind is My Spirit working things out in your life for your good and for My glory. After a while, you will turn around and face the other way. As you do this, you will run with the wind and it will carry you in its power to do My will. You will run with My Spirit and My power will cause you to ride the high places of the earth with Me!

My wind will blow hard in this next season of your life, but don't try to hide from it, **face into it and let it have its perfect work in you.** I love you, My daughter. Perfect love casts out fear.

Be perfected in My love and all fear will be cast out. There is no fear in love! You are being perfected in My love. You are being fashioned and transformed into My image. You will not be destroyed by My wind, only strengthened and perfected. Growth does not come without the wind.

Going Deeper:

This journal entry came one morning about six months before one of the toughest seasons of my life. Little did I know when the Lord spoke this into my heart that before long my husband and I would face winds of adversity as we had never yet experienced. We faced financial hardship, health problems, including two surgeries, the death of my dear mother, unemployment, losing two businesses, and huge debt. I was, indeed, facing the winds of change, but the Lord was right there with me and He worked in my heart, perfecting me in His love, and throughout the entire storm, in the midst of the struggle, there was always peace and strength.

Are you experiencing the winds of adversity in your life right now? Take comfort in knowing that He is at your right hand, too. He is doing His work of cleansing and purifying you so that you will come forth as pure gold.

Suffering and struggle has an important place in living our purpose and fulfilling our destiny. Jesus is our example. He suffered much as He fulfilled His purpose for us, didn't He?

When we persevere through the trials and tribulations of this life, we do grow stronger. They say that if you helped a bird break out of its egg or a butterfly out of its cocoon, it would soon die. It is precisely the struggle to break free that makes it strong enough to fly with its new wings into the next season of life!

Wind is often a symbol of the Holy Spirit in the Bible. In this verse, it is the Hebrew word "ruach" which is often used for God's Spirit and one of the meanings is endowing men with various gifts.

Here we see God comes in and calms the wind and brings them out of their distresses. The actual meaning here is that He leads and guides us out of the storm TO something, toward a purpose and for a result. There are gifts in the wind, even the stormy wind that threatens to destroy us. There is a greater purpose.

So, if facing the wind is a part of God's plan for our lives, then that means that **He is working through it** with us. Look for the gifts in the battle and you will find there are many. The key is to see who you are *becoming* in the midst of the struggle. Then just as Jesus did, you will "see the fruit of the travail of your soul and be satisfied." (see Isaiah 53:11)

I am now facing the other way and running with the wind as it carries me on to do the will of my Father! The gifts that came in the struggle of that season are many and the fruit from the travails of my soul are rich and satisfying! It wasn't easy, but it infused my life with power and strength. You will make it through, too! Consider it all joy, for He is with you in the storm.

You are never alone!

For further reading and meditation:
Song of Solomon 4:16
Isaiah 40:28-31
James 1:2-4
1 Peter 1:6-9
1 Peter 4:12-19

Your Turn: Ask the Lord to speak to you about the winds of adversity in your life. Then record below or in your journal and what He says to you.

8 - FAITH GLASSES

"Things which eye has not seen and ear has not heard and which have not entered the heart of man, all that God has prepared for those who love Him. For to us God revealed them through the Spirit; for the Spirit searches all things, even the depths of God."
1 Corinthians 2:9-10

The Vision:

I saw Jesus standing in front of a lake, His back to me. He was looking out over the lake, off to the horizon, it seems. I moved to His side and He took hold of my hand. He pointed to something far away across the lake. It is then that I noticed the fog or mist covering the lake. It was impossible for me to see what Jesus was pointing to.

He handed me a pair of glasses and said to me, "You must always see with eyes of faith. You cannot clearly see My purposes and My plan for you without eyes of faith."

What are You saying to me, Lord?

He said, "It's always a choice, daughter. Just as you put on your reading glasses and then you can see to read, you must daily choose to walk and see by faith."

So in the vision, I took the glasses and put them on. They seemed to become a part of my face, like they melded into my face. Then the fog began to clear and dissipate, slowly at first.

What struck me as I looked out at the scene before me was the stunning beauty – everything sparkled! Colors were so vibrant! There were mountains and valleys and the beauty of nature, but also cities, buildings, and activity everywhere. It was all so beautiful and spectacular!

The next thing I realized was the vastness of it all! It was so

BIG and so GRAND and so VAST! As far as the eyes could see, but also so high and so deep and so wide! There was absolutely NO LACK!! Richness and abundance were everywhere!

I realized at that moment that Jesus and I were no longer holding hands. His arms were around me and He was holding me so close I was surrounded by His presence and His glory. I was literally IN HIM!

He said, "As you see with eyes of faith what I have provided for you and planned for you, **you must declare what you see daily**! Declare my will over your life. Speak forth what you see, confess the truth over your circumstances - **that I have given you more than enough.** I am abundantly supplying all you need. There is NO LACK in My Kingdom. As you declare what you see with your eyes of faith, it will be established on the earth in your life."

As I looked deeper into the vision, I saw myself picking up one small golden nugget. Out of all the vastness of that rich abundance, it was but a speck. It was about the size of a walnut. As I looked at it, I was filled with the knowledge that this one nugget contained enough provision to wipe out all our financial debt! And that was only a tiny speck out of all that God has for me!

These verses tell us that God "has prepared" things for us. Our natural eyes and ears cannot comprehend those things, but our spirits can, and we will hear and see when we listen to God's Spirit with our spirit eyes and ears. He has made everything ready for us. And God reveals all that He has prepared through His Spirit. He is ready to uncover all that is hidden from our natural senses.

We just need to put on our Faith Glasses. Why do we so often only see lack instead of abundance? It always has to do with where we set our minds – what our eyes are looking at! We see lack when our minds are focused on the lies the enemy puts before us. As Jesus said to me, we always have a choice! We can choose to see through eyes of faith the abundance He has provided and declare that over our lives. Or we can choose to continue to believe the lie that there isn't ever enough.

What do you choose to see?

For further reading and meditation:

Psalm 36:5-9
1 Corinthians 2: 11-16
Ephesians 3:20
Philippians 4:19
2 Peter 1:2-3

Your Turn: Put on your eyes of faith and ask the Lord to show you what He has provided for you. Then record what He speaks to you below or in your journal.

9 - I AM YOUR TREASURE

*"For God, who said, 'Light shall shine out of darkness,' is the One who has shone in our hearts to give the light of the knowledge of the glory of God in the face of Christ. But we have this treasure in earthen vessels, that the surpassing greatness of the power may be of God and not from ourselves." **2 Corinthians 4:6-7***

The Vision:

I was standing with Jesus by a lake with woods on our left side and the lake on our right. He stood in front of me with His hands out toward me, palms up. In His hands were beautiful gemstones of every color imaginable, sparkling in brilliant radiance, and rainbows were coming out of them.

As I looked down at His feet, I realized these gems were coming out of His very Being and they were everywhere, covering the seashore and filling the woods. The trees were made of these gems, the leaves were gems, too. The water of the lake was a crystal sea of glass. Everywhere I looked, I saw the beauty of the gems sparkling and shimmering in the sunlight.

Jesus held out one of these gems to me to inspect closely. He placed it in my hands. It was clear as crystal and perfect in every way. It was as light as air to hold. As I gazed into this gem, I realized I was getting lost in the beauty of it. I could see the full spectrum of color as I looked into the gem. It was as if there was an entire world in just that one gem and I felt as if I were moving or flying into that world! It was thrilling!

Then I realized that every one of those gems was like this one. There were millions of them everywhere, flowing out of Jesus, out of His very Being!

I looked up into His face, so full of love. His eyes are like fire looking deeply into my very soul, warming me to my depths with His love. I was so aware of His love filling me and consuming me.

What are You saying to me, Lord?

I Am your Treasure. Each gem you see is filled with the endless joy and beauty of My Being. My very nature is love, joy, peace, beauty, and wisdom. There is no end to what you can experience in Me.

But sometimes people take only one gem and try to hide it and preserve it and keep it for themselves. They build their lives and doctrines around just one facet of who I Am, one small revelation of My truth, forgetting that it is about Me, it all flows from Me. When they focus on the gem of truth and not on Me, the luster will fade and it will become a hard stone, just as the Israelites found when they tried to hoard My manna and it became foul and worm-infested.

The Life flows from My Father through Me to you. Keep your eyes on Me, not on what I give you. Stay connected to the Life Force itself and all these gems will be yours to enjoy.

Going Deeper:

Have you grasped this amazing truth? That we are vessels, containing the incredible treasure of the power of God? The description of this vision I had in prayer doesn't even come close to capturing this stunning truth! This verse is literally saying that God has deposited into frail, clay pots (us) this power that exceeds way beyond all measure – literally "supereminence" or abundantly, exceedingly far more than any other power.

This power is the word *"dunamis"*, which means inherent power (power residing in something by virtue of its nature). This is God's nature we are talking about here – miracle performing, abundance of provision, the might and strength of hosts of armies – that kind of power. Far beyond what we could ever imagine.

And WE carry this power around inside of us!

45

Why did God place such a treasure in such frail creatures? So that we would all know that this power is of God, not from ourselves. We carry these incredible gems around to shine His light into the darkness of this world. We are to give this light, the light of the knowledge of His glory in the face of Christ, to everyone we meet. And He entrusted YOU with this incredible treasure.

For further reading and meditation:

Ephesians 1:18-23
Ephesians 3:14-21
Colossians 1:9-17

Your Turn: Ask the Lord to show you the amazing treasure He has deposited inside of you and what He wants you to do with it! Then record below or in your journal what He speaks to you.

10 - RIDE WITH ME

*"Yet those who wait for the Lord will gain new strength. They will mount up with wings like eagles, they will run and not get tired, they will walk and not become weary." **Isaiah 40:31***

The Vision:

I'm riding a horse with the Lord (we each have a horse). We are riding side by side on a path through the woods. I am following the Lord at times when the path is narrow and steep as we go up a mountain. We are flying as we ride across open meadows and on the beach through the waves.

What are You saying to me, Lord?

Ride with Me, in sync with Me, always in step with where I am going and what I am doing. Never ride out on your own. The horse is your calling, your mission and My purpose for you in this life. You have been prepared and taught and you have learned to ride well. You are still learning and as you continue to ride in step with Me you will be advancing and taking ground for Me and My Kingdom.

The horse also represents the power and strength of My Spirit in you. You cannot do My works in your own strength; you will soon tire and grow weary just as you would if you were to walk on a long journey. The horse is a very powerful and strong animal and can go much further and faster than a man or a woman on foot.

My Spirit is in you and will carry you everywhere I want you to go. He will be your strength and will empower you to do My will. Ride on the wings of My Spirit and let Me carry you wherever I want to take you. Your circumstances are My concern and by My design. Do not worry about them.

Going Deeper:

In this scripture, the phrase "gain new strength" actually means **to make an exchange.** It means that we trade in our strength, might, and power for His. Some versions use the word "renew," but it is literally "new" strength because it is not our own at all! We make a holy exchange and take on the strength of the One who never grows weary – whose power is unsurpassed in the entire universe. I'd say, that's a pretty good deal!

Have you ever tried to step out ahead of God and start doing things in your own power? It is much harder, isn't it? It feels like you're swimming upstream – it feels like you're striving. And it leaves you exhausted and drained in every way – physically, emotionally, mentally and spiritually. Why do we do this if it's so hard? Usually, because we are so impatient!

But when we move with God and in the power of His Spirit, in His timing, and in His way – it feels like FLOW! It feels effortless and powerful, even when we're working hard. At the end of the day, we're energized even when we are physically tired. Have you experienced this?

Jesus is our perfect example. He said that He could do **nothing** on His own initiative! **NOTHING!!** He only did what He saw the Father doing. If that is true about Jesus, why should we think we can do things on our own?

Remember, those that **wait on the Lord** will gain NEW strength – His strength. Do you hate to wait? Most of us do. So, think about this. The word for "wait" in this verse comes from a root word meaning to *"bind together by twisting."* This kind of waiting is not where you're on your own, waiting alone for someone to come along. Instead, you are bound together with the Lord as one and you are eagerly expecting and looking for His next move with hope. That's what this word literally means here!

So the next time you feel that impatience and are tempted to move out on your own, imagine yourself sitting on a Holy Spirit horse with the Lord by your side and you are watching for His next move with eager anticipation because you know when He starts to move, you will move with Him and **you'll be going for the ride of your life!**

For further reading and meditation:

Psalm 103:5
Isaiah 41:10
John 5:19
John 16:13-15
Galatians 6:9

Your Turn: Ask the Lord to show you how to ride with Him! Then, as you tune to flow, write below or in your journal what He speaks to you.

11 - THE LIVING RIVER

"If any man is thirsty, let him come to Me and dink. He who believes in Me, as the Scripture said, 'From his innermost being shall flow rivers of living water.'" **John 7:37-38**

The Vision:

I see a wooded scene with a pure, sparkling river rushing through it. It is alive! It's filled with life and joy and it's like the water is jumping up with sheer joy as it runs over rocks and runs through the land. Everything around this river is so alive, so green, so filled with joy. The trees are lifting their branches up toward heaven like they are praising God. There's a song coming from the river and from all the trees and plants and animals. It's so happy and bright! The squirrels and chipmunks are playing together! Fish are leaping in and out of the water in a kind of dance! Oh, the life! The scene is teeming with life!

A little girl enters the scene. She is wearing a dress, about 8 or 9 years old. She is looking around at everything, marveling. She starts to twirl around, letting her dress billow out as she spins in delight. She is dancing, twirling, spinning! Laughing in pure joy and delight! She sits at the edge of the river, takes her shoes off and dips her feet in the river. Oh, what bliss! The river sends thrills through her body, refreshing and renewing her to the depths of her soul. She wants more, wants to go all the way in, but the river is rushing so fast and she is afraid. Where will it take me? Will I get hurt or even die? Is it okay?

Oh, it feels so good! Like nothing she's ever experienced before. Like nothing I've ever experienced before! I want more! I want to go all the way in, Lord! I suddenly realize that I'm the little girl sitting by the river.

Jesus sits down next to me and takes my hand in His. He looks deeply into my eyes, to my very soul. His eyes are pure love, fire, searching, but so pure I can get lost in them.

He searches my very depths and covers me with such love!

What are You saying to me, Lord?

The river is Me, My Spirit inside you. I am with you, do not be afraid. Me in you and you in Me. We are one. Where I go, you go. Where you go, I go. But you are still holding back, My daughter. The cares of this world burden you and distract you - they keep you from Me. This need not be so. Don't hold any part of yourself back from Me. Give Me your whole self. Come near to Me, nearer than you've ever come before. All I have is yours. You can be completely filled and overflowing with this same joy that your feet are experiencing. **This joy is meant to fill you completely.**

I asked: How do I give myself to You completely, Lord? How do I go totally into the River? I want to be like Mary and sit at Your feet, choosing the ONE thing that I need – You and Your Word.

He answered: You said it, my child. **It is a choice!** As soon as you wake up, CHOOSE to step into the River of My Spirit and I will show you how to live out of the River, even in the daily grind. It will no longer be a "grind" – your day-to-day life will take on the luster and sparkle of the scene I have shown you. Everyone who comes into contact with you will feel it and sense it and be drawn to the River, too. Let Me bring My Life through your life. I will do it. It is My work, not yours. Just make your life available to My Spirit. Choose the River each day. Give yourself to Me every day, holding nothing back, and I will do things in you and through you that you cannot even imagine!

Going Deeper:

What a powerful truth! **We always have the choice to live out of that river of life and joy!** The tense of the verbs "come and drink" here is one of continual, repeated action. Jesus was literally saying, *"Let him keep coming and let him keep drinking."* Just as He invited the woman at the well to drink of this living water, He invites us to come and drink continually, every day, every moment.

This living water is His Spirit, Who lives inside of us, in our innermost being. This is the same living water Isaiah spoke about, which would continually guide us, satisfy our soul in scorched places, and give strength to our bones. He said we would be like a well-watered garden.

Will you choose to drink from this River today?

For further reading and meditation:

Psalm 36:8
Isaiah 44:3
Isaiah 55:1
Isaiah 58:11
John 4:10, 14

Your Turn: Ask the Lord to show you how to continually drink from this river and how to stay in its flow. Then, write down what He says to you below or in your journal.

12 - THE FRAGRANCE OF A FOCUSED HEART

"But the Lord answered and said to her, 'Martha, Martha, you are worried and bothered about so many things; but only a few things are necessary, really only one, for Mary has chosen the good part, which shall not be taken away from her.'" **Luke 10:41-42**

The Vision:

As I read this passage, the scene became very real to me. It was as if I was there, standing against a wall, observing and taking it all in. The first thing I noticed was the energy in the room. It felt frantic, hurried, and chaotic. The room was packed with people and it was loud. People were shouting and demanding to be served.

Then I saw Martha, scurrying about trying to keep everyone happy. She was drenched in sweat, her face was red hot and her hair was matted to her face and head. Her eyes were filled with fear and even anger and she looked exhausted. She sent hateful stares toward her sister, Mary, who sat quietly at the feet of Jesus, completely focused on Him, totally unaware of anyone else in the room.

As my gaze rested on Mary, I was fascinated by the expression on her face. I don't think I have ever seen such peace and contentment! Her face glowed with an inner light and I felt an incredible longing to be where she was – to be in that same place of utter calm and serenity. Her eyes never left the face of Jesus. It was like she was in a bubble with just the two of them. Nothing else mattered in that moment to her.

How often I am like Martha, so bothered and distracted by things that are not really necessary or even important! My heart longs to be like Mary, with a laser-like focus on the only thing that I really need – Jesus. But my head gets in the way. So I asked the Lord about this passage and to teach me how to be more like Mary. **What are You saying to me, Lord?**

The difference between Mary and Martha in this story is focus. **It's a matter of where you are focusing your eyes (the eyes of your heart).** Mary's heart was completely turned to Me and that is all she was aware of in that room. She only saw and heard Me because as she centered all of her heart on me, everything else faded away.

She found the secret place of My presence. She heard My heartbeat and felt My breath upon her. She received My life into her innermost being. All she cared about was bringing pleasure to Me.

Martha was not focused on Me, but on herself and how she was serving Me. **She was focused on doing, not being.** She was not close to Me, so she could not hear My words or sense My desire for her to be completely surrendered only to Me. She could not understand Mary and only perceived Mary to be "wasting" her time just sitting at My feet.

That is how it is when you are distracted by the cares of the world or the details of your daily life. When you are not centered on Me, concerned only with ministering to My pleasure in the midst of your day to day tasks, then you will feel far from me and you will easily be encumbered by the cares of your life. They will drag you down and your heart will be troubled and not at peace. If you will take the position Mary took and place your heart at My feet, focused on pleasing Me as your first priority each and every moment, your heart will be at peace. Set your mind and heart on Me and I will keep you in perfect peace. That is the one thing you need and it is all you need.

Think of yourself as an alabaster jar. You are an earthen vessel that contains a very precious and costly perfume, your heart – the innermost part of you. Your flesh and your soul are the vessels containing your spirit, the heart of who you are. When you are willing to "break" that jar by subjecting your soul and flesh to My Spirit and pouring out your very essence on Me, then the fragrance of a surrendered soul fills the air and brings Me so much pleasure. When it no longer matters to you what others think or say about this "wasting" of yourself on Me, you will find that your life is anointing Me with this costly perfume and the fragrance of it will fill the atmosphere around you. Everyone that comes into contact with you will sense it. Some will be drawn to Me because of it, others will become indignant and offended, even some Christians who are still "Martha's" and don't understand.

This is what I desire most, however, from My Bride, My Church. **Undivided focus of heart, mind, soul** – a pouring out of the very life unto Me in abandonment. Out of that place of surrender, you will be a channel and a vessel of My life flow which will be effective and powerful and will accomplish much more than the service of the distracted and burdened "Martha's". Only one thing is needed and you must choose daily. It is a matter of focus. Where are the eyes of your heart focused, moment by moment?

Going Deeper:

Consider where these two women positioned themselves in the presence of Jesus. They both loved Him, there's no doubt about that. But Martha allowed herself to be distracted with her serving. The word for "distracted" in the Greek here means **to draw away** and the root of this word literally has the picture of **dragging all around with cares.** It's the picture of being burdened and encumbered. I sure know that feeling, don't you?

She was too busy and over-occupied *with things* that don't really matter and that drew her away from the **ONE THING** that does matter! Of course we need to take care of the daily tasks of living, but when we take that to an extreme, we become like Martha. And then we get bothered when we see the freedom and peace of people like Mary. We get jealous and want them to share in our worries and burdens.

But Jesus corrected Martha and literally told her she was "worried and bothered about so many things." The words He used literally mean that she was anxious and troubled in her mind about many, many things. He pointed out that she really only needed one thing and that it was a matter of choice. **Mary had chosen that one thing.**

The word used for "chosen" here means **to pick out for one's self out of many options** and it is in the middle voice. The middle voice is when something is offered and you then have to act to receive it, like a gift. It's your choice whether or not to take what is offered to you.

We are all offered this same gift, this opportunity to choose the one thing we really need – sitting at the feet of Jesus, hearing His word. Mary had the same options Martha had in that moment, but she picked out for herself the one thing, the only thing, that really matters. She not only listened to His word, but she heard it, meaning that she attended to His word, considered what He said, and then understood and learned from what she heard.

In John's version of this story, we also see her taking very costly perfume and anointing His feet, wiping them with her hair. The room was filled with the fragrance of her devotion and worship. Everyone in the room was affected by her focused heart. It changed the very atmosphere.

This is the choice we have every single day. To fill the room with the fragrance of a heart focused on the only thing that matters and therefore draw attention to Jesus or be anxious and bothered by so many things that weigh us down and draw us away from His presence and His peace.

What choice will you make today?

For further reading and meditation:

John 12:1-8
Psalm 27:4-6
2 Corinthians 2:14-15

Your Turn: Ask the Lord to show you how to choose the ONE thing you need today. Then record below or in your journal what He speaks to you.

13 - THE BRIDGE

"Do not fear, for I am with you. Do not anxiously look about you, for I am your God, I will strengthen you, surely, I will help you. Surely I will uphold you with My righteous right hand."
Isaiah 41:10

The Vision:

I am in the woods by a stream. It's very cool and shaded, not much light coming in, but the atmosphere is one of rest, refreshing and relaxation. It's beautiful and peaceful. I am lying down, resting peacefully. I see a bridge over the stream and on the other side it is much darker and denser. Jesus is standing on the bridge on my side, leaning against the railing, looking at me. He wants me to come to Him and go with Him over the bridge to the other side, but I don't want to. I am content where I am. His eyes are so full of love, no condemnation or impatience, just kindness and compassion, but still He is persistent. I should come to Him.

So I get up and go to Him. He takes my hands in His and looks me full in the face. His love washes over me and fills me up completely. It's like being under a shower of joy unspeakable!

What are You saying to me, Lord?

I will never leave you. I will never forsake you. No matter what you encounter on the other side of this bridge, know that this is true and will never, ever change. I am taking you places you have never been before in the Spirit and it will be like walking in a dark forest at times where you can't see where your next step is going to be, but I am with you and I am in you. It is only dark because it is unknown. There is nothing to fear and the evil one cannot touch you there because you are in My will. You are in Me, the secret place of My presence.

Rise up, My daughter, My cherished one, and come with Me. Do not be complacent or comfortable where you are now. It's a new season for you. It is a season of power in My Spirit, a season of grace, a season of dying to self and living to Me. It won't be easy, especially for your flesh, but it will be glorious!

Don't be afraid, don't be timid, don't hold back, don't hesitate. When I speak, you must speak. When I sing, you must sing. When I cry, you must cry. When I laugh, you must laugh. Lay aside your own expectations, your own agenda, your own ambitions. This is not about you, but it is about Me in you, Me and you, together walking out My purposes in your life. It is about glorifying Me and doing the work of our Father. It is a journey and an adventure and it will be worth it all when you receive the glory and the treasure stored up for you! So, come on, let's go!

Going Deeper:

How often in our walk with God do we encounter bridges like this one? To me, bridges represent change – a transition to a new season. It's not easy to leave the comfort zone, where things are familiar and peaceful, like in this vision. The other side of the bridge looks dark and ominous because it is unknown.

But Jesus calls us to trust Him. His promise to be with us always never changes. In this verse, the phrase "anxiously look about you" carries the feeling of bewilderment. It's the picture of someone looking all around for help in fear and dismay. There is no need for that with God. He is with us. He is always right here, no matter where that is.

He not only promises to be with us, He also promises to strengthen, help, and uphold us with His right hand. Let's look at each of these words.

Strengthen: This word means to be brave and courageous, to prevail and be secure and established. No matter what is on the other side of the bridge, we can be assured that His strength will give us courage and we will be established in that new place and season where He leads us.

Help: This word means to surround, protect, and aid. He is not only with us, but we are surrounded by His presence, like a shield of protection. I picture this as being inside a bubble – being IN Him, safe and secure.

Uphold with My righteous right hand: The right hand in Scripture means the strongest side. To uphold means to hold fast and support. He holds us fast. We are in His strong right hand where He is holding on to us! You can't get any more secure than that!

And His righteousness is whatever is just and right and true. We can be sure that no matter what we walk into on that dark side of the bridge, He will justify us and bring us deliverance and victory, even when things seem unfair or unjust. As long as we trust Him and walk with Him in every new season, our feet will land on solid ground.

For further reading and meditation:

Deut. 31:6-8
Joshua 1:5
Psalm 118:5-6
Hebrews 13:5-6

So, my friend, what bridges are you facing today?

Your Turn: Ask Him to show you how present He is with you now and will be as you cross that bridge to the other side. Write down all that He speaks to your heart below or in your journal.

14 - THE FIERY FOUNTAIN

"Therefore, behold, I will allure her, bring her into the wilderness, and speak kindly to her. Then I will give her vineyards from there, and the valley of Achor as a door of hope. And she will sing there as in the days of her youth, as in the day when she came up from the land of Egypt." **Hosea 2:14-15**

The Vision:

I was standing next to a very small spring bubbling up out of the ground. After a short while, it suddenly sputtered and disappeared as it was sucked back underground. The earth was totally dry for some time until, without warning, a huge pillar of water blasted up from the ground, shooting high into the air and becoming a massive and fiery fountain! As I looked closely, I noticed that there was fire in the water! It burned with intensity and a purity I had never seen before. This "fire-water" spread out in all directions as it hit the ground, while the fountain continued to surge high into the air.

What are You saying to me, Lord?

This fiery fountain represents different seasons in your life. There was a time when your influence and power to touch lives was quite small in its reach, confined to those closest to you. This was followed by a dry season, a wilderness of the soul, during which you went into the secret place with Me, in hidden places where there was no outward manifestation of My work within you. This was after you had experienced deep wounding from people you loved and trusted and this caused you to withdraw into the wilderness.

During this wilderness season, I worked deep things into your spirit, purifying and refining your heart so that you could come to the place where your only need and your deepest desire was just to dwell in My presence. The desire or need to be approved by others began to fade away as the revelation of your immense worth and value to Me and to this world began to be established in your soul and became crystal clear.

The seeds of confidence were sown into your heart as your soul grew strong. As My deeper work created a greater foundation deep inside you, My power intensified until the time came for it to be released.

I whispered to your heart that the deeper you are rooted in My love, the greater will be the power of My love in you to touch others. You have traveled through this season of preparation, my daughter, and now you are entering a season of release and much fruit. You now have more compassion for the broken and hurting, and this fountain from your soul will refresh the weary.

Going Deeper:

Have you ever been drawn into the wilderness by the Lord? At first, we often don't recognize it as an invitation from the Lord to a deep season of growth. At first, it just looks and feels like troubled times, it feels like hurt and pain and as in my case, betrayal and rejection. That's what the valley of Achor is - a low time in your life where there is trouble and disturbance. The word "Achor" literally means **troubled**. The root word is "akar" – to trouble, stir up, disturb, make someone taboo (rejection), calamity.

Sometimes when trouble comes into our lives, the Lord will use those times to call us into the wilderness for a special encounter with Him. He doesn't cause the disturbance or trouble, but He does work through it for our good!

In this passage, the word "allure" actually means **to be open, spacious, and wide.** He doesn't bring us into a scary, dark, barren place – it's not that kind of wilderness. This is a place of opening and spaciousness to receive so much more revelation and understanding than we have ever experienced before. This is a pivotal time of powerful growth in our innermost being!

And when He says that he "brings her into the wilderness," this is the most beautiful picture of His love. It means that He leads us and even carries us away to this open place. The word for "wilderness" is actually **pasture**, a place of nourishment and rest. The root for this word means **to speak**. He nourishes us in this pastureland with His words of love. The image here is of Him singing over us!

And then He "speaks kindly" to you there, literally meaning that **He speaks to your heart**. He speaks and sings His love into the very depths of your soul and you are transformed there in that wild and wonderful place. There are gifts here - fruitfulness and a door of hope – an opening into new seasons where you will sing as in the days of your youth – with new life and joyfulness!

For further reading and meditation:

Song of Songs 2:10-14
Hosea 2:14-23
Psalm 91
John 10:2-4
Romans 8:28

Your Turn: Ask the Lord to speak to you about your wilderness season and the gifts He has for you in this special place. Then record below or in your journal what He says to you.

15 - WINEPRESS WORSHIP

"Though the fig tree should not blossom, and there be no fruit on the vines, though the yield of the olive should fail, and the fields produce no food, though the flock should be cut off from the fold, and there be no cattle in the stalls; Yet, I will exult in the Lord, I will rejoice in the God of my salvation. The Lord God is my strength. He has made my feet like hinds' feet, and He makes me walk on my high places." **Habakkuk 3:17-19**

The Vision:

I was worshiping the Lord in church when I saw a winepress. It looked like a large cylindrical shaped vat. The sides and top were pressing down and in with great pressure. Then I saw wine begin oozing out through the sides and out from under the lid.

What are You saying to me, Lord?

The sweetest wine to Me is the wine of praise and worship that is offered up to Me when you are in the winepress. When the circumstances of life are pressing in on you from all sides and you feel the weight of it, yet you still praise Me. When it seems that all is lost and there is nothing left to give, and you wonder how you can possibly endure this trial, and yet you still offer your heart to Me in worship, it is the sweetest of wines to Me, and it pleases Me more than you could ever imagine.

It is easy to praise Me when life is good and everything is going your way. But the good times do not test your faith; it is in the trials and battles that your faith is tested and purified. When you are facing challenges and difficulties, hurt and loss, disappointment and pain, and yet can still look up to Me and give your heart to Me in worship, My heart is thrilled beyond measure!

So do not fear the winepress or rail against it. Let it do its work in you by bringing you to a place of utter dependence on Me. And in that place of death to self, offer up the sacrifice of praise and thanksgiving before My throne, even though you feel you cannot. My Spirit in you will bring forth that sweet wine of pure worship if you will only yield and surrender all to Me.

This is the worship that brings Me pleasure and glory. This is also what will bring you victory! When you praise me while you are in the winepress, your enemy cannot stand it and he will flee!

My strength is made perfect in your weakness and My power will rise up within you and cause you to go to a higher place, above the storms raging around you, and you will be able to walk through the trial in power, giving Me glory and honor!

Going Deeper:

It's called the **sacrifice of praise** for a reason, right? Sometimes the hardest thing to do in the midst of a trial and difficulty is to lift up our hearts in praise and worship. That's usually the last thing we feel like doing when we're feeling pressed in from all sides, when everything is going wrong and it looks like all is lost. But that's exactly the BEST time to worship!

Winepress worship is the sweetest to God! And this type of worship is not passive! The words "exult" and "rejoice" are full of passionate praise! The picture here is to triumph and jump for joy! This is worship that is full of faith and hope, trusting that God is bringing us the victory through the darkest hour! How could that NOT please the heart of God?

And look at the gifts that are waiting there - the strength of the Lord comes flooding in to carry us through the storm. And then He makes our feet like hinds' feet with the amazing ability to walk on high places! The word for "high places" here means **mountains** (which often symbolize huge problems and obstacles), but it also can mean **battlefield**! And this is not merely "walking" like a leisurely stroll! This is a **treading down in victory** kind of walking! This is taking those treacherous, rocky slops with sure and swift steps.

Have you ever watched a deer walk up a mountainside? They actually bound and leap without fear because their feet are created to handle that kind of ground!

Winepress worship releases that into our spirits. So, the next time you feel squeezed from every side, stop and offer the sacrifice of winepress worship. Jump for joy and exult in your God! Bless the Lord with the sweetest of wines and know that He is with you and will give you the victory!

For further reading and meditation:

Psalm 28:7
Psalm 118:1-15
2 Corinthians 4:7-18
2 Corinthians 12:9
Philippians 4:4-7

Your Turn: Ask the Lord to show you what it means to Him when you worship Him in the midst of your winepress. Record what He says to you below or in your journal.

16 - TWO WELLS

"Everyone who drinks of this water shall thirst again, but whoever drinks of the water that I shall give him shall never thirst; but the water that I shall give him shall become in him a well of water springing up to eternal life." **John 4:13-14**

The Vision:

I saw a woman standing before two wells. She was weeping. She looked from one well to the other, back and forth, clearly struggling with which one to choose. Jesus sat near the well on her right, watching and waiting, His hand outstretched toward her.

What are You saying to me, Lord?

There are two wells from which to draw water for your soul. One is from the earth. These waters will satisfy you for a little while, but you will soon find yourself thirsty again and unfulfilled. I Am the other well, the well of living water, the fountain of Life. When you come to Me to drink of this living water, you will be satisfied to the depths of your soul. When you drink of Me, you will find that you have an inner strength and power that refreshes you in every season, whether plenty or famine. My well never runs dry! You can draw from Me continuously and you will never be thirsty for the earthly, worldly waters again.

You have tried to fill your soul with water from the world's well. You have hewn for yourself broken cisterns that cannot hold water and that is why you keep coming back to this feeling of emptiness, loneliness, and despair. I am talking about relationships. Trying to fill your soul with the waters from earthly relationships does not satisfy. These relationships are like broken cisterns. They cannot sustain you or fulfill you or satisfy you. I know your innermost thoughts and desires. I see the deep pain and hurt, the loneliness and despair of your soul.

I know you intimately and love you everlastingly. There is no love greater than the love I want to pour into your soul if you will only come to Me and drink of Me. Draw from the well of everlasting Life and you will find what your heart is longing for. This is the only way to live on the earth. You are destined to be a source of life for others as I fill your soul with My life. Then you can love others the way you were meant to love and the way you were meant to be loved – with the source of My Life springing up within you.

Come to Me and drink and be satisfied. Come to Me with your hurting heart and place the pieces of your life in My hands. I am waiting for you. I am longing to fill you with My love, with the waters of true life and true love. I will make all things new in your life if you will allow Me, if you will choose to draw from Me. I have prepared things for you that you cannot even imagine; things that will bring you joy beyond measure.

I am near, only a whisper away.

Going Deeper:

We always have a choice. And it is a daily choice. Just as this woman in John 4 went to the well daily to draw her water, we choose each day which well to draw from to nourish our soul and spirit.

In the Bible, wells and cisterns represent relationships. Jesus tells us that when we draw from His well, that water satisfies every need. In fact, when you look deeper into the meaning of the word for "well" here, it is the picture of flowing water or a fountain that springs up. It is not stagnant water that sits there. It flows, it leaps up, it gushes forth! It is *living water* and it gives us eternal life – life without beginning and ending. This is life that has always been and will always be – never ceasing, everlasting.

In contrast, the other well is a cistern, which is a holding tank for water. The water there is not alive or flowing and it does not satisfy for long. In fact, it is broken. It can't hold water for long. The choice is a fountain that gushes forth with everlasting life or a broken cistern that can't hold onto what is poured into it for long.

It's the picture of two relationships. A relationship with Jesus, the Lover of our souls, who gives us everything our souls long for or a relationship with the world that entices us with empty, broken promises and cannot ever fully satisfy. Just like the woman in this vision, it is always our choice.

For further reading and meditation:

Jeremiah 2:13
John 4:4-14
John 7:38
1 Corinthians 2:9

Your Turn: Ask the Lord to speak to you about the living water He has for you today. Then record what He says to you below or in your journal.

17 - THE MUSHROOM TREE

"And he will be like a tree firmly planted by streams of water, which yields its fruit in its season, and its leaf does not wither; and in whatever he does, he prospers." **Psalm 1:3**

The Vision:

I see a huge tree shaped somewhat like a mushroom or triangle. The branches are full of bright green leaves that seem to dance with life as they reach out wide in all directions and the top of the tree is pointed at the top, stretching high into the sky. They are heavy with luscious fruit. The trunk is massive and radiates with strength, confidence, and deep wisdom. The bark is smooth and all the branches are perfectly straight.

What are You saying to me, Lord?

This tree represents the person who has allowed Me full access in their life. They have allowed Me to do the work in them that I am anointed to do. They become rooted, steadfast, immovable. Their faith is strong and has grown through each season in life to become this massive trunk; strong enough to support the growth of this huge tree. And it can drink deeply of the richness and depths of My wisdom and truth because the roots go down so deep.

There are no rocks in the soil of their heart because they have allowed Me to remove the lies they were believing and to reveal the false conclusions and sins that had been hindrances in their lives and prevented the truth to go deep and take root. Once the rocks were removed and the soil prepared, My truth took root and went deep, causing the massive growth. This tree is a planting of the Lord. It is a life lived in and through Me, glorifying Me. It can withstand any storm or drought. It cannot be moved.

The tree points heavenward because that is its home and it keeps its focus on things above. That's the true destination and where it always yearns to go.

This is one who knows what her true destiny is: to live forever in the presence of God.

The triangular shape of the branches shows that it is reaching outward always as it stretches and points upward. It reaches out to offer its strength and shade to others. This life is not lived to please itself, but to draw others to the truth. It is a place of safety, security and rest to the weary and hope to the hopeless and fearful ones. But even as it is giving out, it still always draws from the Source of Life through its deep roots and then always looking up and keeping its eyes fixed on Me.

The bark is smooth and straight as are the limbs. There are no entanglements or thorns to distract or deter it from its purpose. The things of the world have been cast off and no longer can become attached to this life. The leaves are lush and very green and full. They are for the healing of the nations, and they are the fruit of this life. They bring life and healing to others, nourishment and refreshing - the crown of a life lived in deep relationship with Me. The fruit grows effortlessly from the Source of Life that this tree feeds from, which is My Life. The person this tree represents can't produce the fruit in herself. It only comes from being one with Me.

Going Deeper:

Who will be like a tree? The man or woman whose delight is in the law of the Lord, who meditates in His law (word) day and night. The person who allows Him full access into their lives. The one who drinks deeply from the living water.

What can this person expect? Blessings, fruitfulness, stability, strength, prosperity, life. Intimacy with the Lord, being known and seen by Him. A life of peace, joy, and love.

For further reading and meditation:

Psalm 1:1-6
Isaiah 61:3
Jeremiah 17:7-8
John 15:1-11
Colossians 1:13

Your Turn: Ask the Lord to show you any place in your life where you have not allowed Him full access, any place where you are not delighting and meditating in His word. Then record below or in your journal all that He speaks to you.

18 - DANCE OF THE BUTTERFLIES

"But we all, with unveiled face beholding as in a mirror the glory of the Lord, are being transformed into the same image from glory to glory, just as from the Lord, the Spirit." **2 Corinthians 3:18**

The Vision:

I saw a meadow full of butterflies, many kinds and colors, rising up into the air and swooping back down over the meadow in a kind of dance. Their movements were smooth and fluid; they moved as one. Then they began flitting from flower to flower and as they opened their wings, their brilliant colors and unique patterns were displayed in all their glory. This butterfly dance was mesmerizing!

What are You saying to me, Lord?

The metamorphosis of a butterfly is the picture of the transformation of a soul into a son or daughter of God. The larva eats and eats, then forms a chrysalis where the creature rests for a season, while it is transformed into a beautiful butterfly. It has to work hard to break out of the chrysalis, and as it does, it becomes stronger so that once it is free, it can spread its wings and fly. This is its destiny.

So it is with you and all of my children. As you feed on my Word, you take in My Life. Then there are seasons where I call you into a hidden place to rest. These are seasons of great change and transformation where My Word that is implanted in your soul and spirit does its deeper work in you. During this season, I speak to your heart and show you who you truly are. As you see My glory, as you gaze upon My truth, you are transformed from glory to glory. You begin to reflect more and more of Me in your very being. You go from strength to strength.

Once that work is complete, I call you back out into the world, now with new wings and colors and brilliance to shine forth My glory through your unique beauty.

Now you are free to fly and fulfill your destiny. You are invited to the dance of the butterflies, displaying the glory of the Lord to all the world!

Going Deeper:

I received this vision and word during a time of great growth and change in my life. I now realize that this type of season is not a one-time deal for us. As we walk with the Lord, there will be many seasons like this – being called to rest while He works more transformation into us, then coming back out to fly some more. This is a continual process, a dance with the Lord. As we behold His glory, we are changed more and more into His likeness and we radiate more and more of His glory out to the world.

We are not yet what we shall be; we are in the process of becoming just like Him. The secret here is this phrase: "with unveiled face beholding as in a mirror the glory of the Lord." As we keep our eyes fixed on His glory, without any masks, but with an open face and heart, we will be gazing at ourselves in this mirror, because we will be like Him. As we behold Him, we will look just like Him, transformed and reflecting His glory to the world.

We are called to the dance of the butterflies. I hope you dance!

For further reading and meditation:

Romans 12:1-16
Colossians 3:1-5
Philippians 3:7-21
1 John 3:1-3

Your Turn: Ask the Lord to show you how He is transforming you from glory to glory. Then record what He speaks to you below or in your journal.

19 - INVITATION TO REST

"Come to Me, all who are weary and heavy-laden and I will give you rest. Take My yoke upon you and learn from Me, for I am gentle and humble in heart, and you shall find rest for your souls; for My yoke is easy and My burden is light." **Matthew 11:28-30**

The Vision:

I was standing in the midst of a swirling wind, like a tornado that had engulfed me. I looked around in confusion at the chaos, trying to figure out how to make sense of it. It was dark, noisy, chaotic. I was paralyzed and could not move.

Suddenly an opening began to form at the top of the swirl and light began to peek through. As I looked up, the opening grew wider and wider, until I saw a rope being lowered into the swirl. I grabbed the rope and instantly I found myself lying on a raft in the middle of a peaceful, serene lake. I looked to my right and realized that Jesus was there next to me on another raft, lying down with His arms behind His head, eyes closed, smiling and soaking up the sun! Our rafts were connected by a silver cord. The lake was perfectly still, like a sheet of glass, even though there was a soft, gentle breeze caressing our faces. Birds were singing incredibly beautiful tunes all around us. I sank into my soft, cozy raft and let all my concerns and worries melt away. It felt like pure bliss – a heavenly peace beyond comprehension.

As I rested there with Jesus in absolute peace, I became aware that we were moving – gliding is more like it. Smoothly, almost imperceptibly, through the water in a definite direction. I opened my eyes to see a silver cord attached to our rafts floating up into the sky. Then I saw that it was attached to a bright star. The star was pulling us toward a narrow path on the other side of the lake.

What are You saying to me, Lord?

This is an invitation to rest, to step into a place of ease and flow.

This has always been the design of life – to remain in flow and ease. You simply remain connected to Me, your source of life and peace.

The swirl you found yourself in represents stress, which is simply the result of being disconnected from Me. Life becomes a load you were not meant to carry. You were designed to experience life in flow, connected to Me, the Source of all You need.

This is an invitation to rest. The rope was lowered into the swirl as an invitation. You grabbed the rope in response and instantly found yourself in My rest, connected to Me. My rest is not inactivity, rather it is literally "going with the flow." You move forward, but with ease and peace, instead of striving and under pressure, which causes stress.

When you are in flow with Me, our work together will flow. I will lead you in the path I have designed for you and the work is joyful and light. This is My invitation to rest. Take My yoke upon you and learn from Me.

Going Deeper:

What an amazing invitation! He says "come" and in that one word, there is so much passion and meaning. It is an urgent calling: "Come here!" He has something far better for us in this life than the scrapping, fighting, striving, stressful chaos that we call life! All that struggle makes us weary and loads us up with burdens too heavy to carry!

But He is calling us to rest! His invitation is not a command here. The phrase "take My yoke" implies that we willingly take it upon ourselves. It is our choice to answer the invitation and grab the rope offered to us. His yoke is easy, which means "fit for use, good, mild, pleasant, kind." It is a perfect fit for us! His burden is light – quick, agile, not weighing us down.

What will we find in this rest? We will discover what it is that our souls long for. We will learn how to walk in the Spirit, in gentleness and humility. We will come to understand what life in the Spirit truly is, we will come to know Him more deeply, and we will find what it is we have always been seeking: true peace, contentment, fulfillment in the depths of our souls.

For further reading and meditation:

Jeremiah 31:25
Psalm 23:1-3
John 15:1-11

Your Turn: Ask the Lord to show you where His invitation to rest is showing up in your life. Then record below or in your journal what He speaks to you.

20 - LEAPING ON MOUNTAINS

*"But in all these things we overwhelmingly conquer through Him who loved us. For I am convinced that neither death, nor life, nor angels, nor principalities, nor things present, nor things to come, nor powers, nor height, nor depth, nor any other created thing, shall be able to separate us from the love of God, which is in Christ Jesus our Lord." **Romans 8:37-39***

The Vision:

I'm leaping from mountaintop to mountaintop with the Lord, effortlessly and joyously. At each peak, we stop and take it all in – the sunrise, the majesty of all we see, vast and endless beauty and grandeur laid out before us, all at our feet. Then we leap (more like a flying leap) to the next peak, with strength, agility, and grace.

What are You saying to me, Lord?

You've got this! The victory is yours! In Me, you have all that you need. You have overcome and will continue to more than overcome all the obstacles the enemy puts in your way. They are nothing to Me.

From the ground (in your own strength), they look like huge insurmountable barriers, but from this viewpoint up here with Me (where you are seated with Me in heavenly places), they are only the landing places for our feet. Nothing is impossible with Me, nothing is insurmountable!

You are more than a conqueror. You are already walking in victory! It's time to take it all in – to see it and to enjoy it! Receive and walk in all that I have given you, all that I have brought you through. All this that you see from the mountaintops is yours, My beautiful one! You already have the Kingdom of God, My cherished one.

All that I have is yours!

Because you are My daughter,
Because you are loved,
Because you are Mine,
Because I love you.

Going Deeper:

The truth is that we already ARE more than conquerors through Him. In this passage in Romans, in the Greek, this means "to gain a surpassing victory, to vanquish beyond, to gain a decisive victory."

But do we believe this truth? Do we SEE it? What stood out to me the most as I saw and heard this message from the Lord was the vast and grand view of it all below us. We are already there on top of the mountains with Him because of His great love for us. We only need to open our eyes and see it all from THAT perspective!

In Him, we are leaping over all the troubles in this world. The obstacles in our way are merely footstools for His feet. And since we are seated with Him in heavenly places, **they are also under our feet.**

If you are having a difficult time seeing that you have the victory now, change your perspective from on the ground to your heavenly position where you are seated with Him far above it all.

For further reading and meditation:

Song of Songs 2:8
Isaiah 52:7-10
Ephesians 2: 6-7
1 John 5:4-5

Your Turn: Ask the Lord to give you His perspective from the mountaintop right now, from your place with Him in heavenly places. Then record what He shows you and speaks to you below or in your journal.

ABOUT THE AUTHOR

Janelle Anderson is a Certified Professional Coach and holds a PCC credential from the International Coach Federation. She is currently working toward completing her Master's degree in Spiritual Counseling with Christian Leadership University (CLU) and is a Communion with God Seminar Facilitator for How to Hear God's Voice as well as a Personal Spiritual Trainer with Communion with God Ministries and CLU.

Janelle is the founder and owner of **Emerging Life Coaching,** where she works with women ready to discover their truest selves and step into the unique destiny God has for them in this life. She leads them through a process of self-discovery and helps them create a plan of action so they can move from where they are to where they want (and are called) to be.

If you or your group would like to learn how to hear God's voice, Janelle is available as a facilitator for **How to Hear God's Voice** seminars. She also teaches a seminar called **Discovering Your Unique Destiny,** where she leads women through a process of self-discovery so they can identify their true life's calling and unique destiny. Janelle also works with women through her individual private coaching practice. To fill out a coaching request form, visit http://www.emerginglifecoaching.com/work-with-me.html

For booking information or to connect with Janelle, see below:

Website: www.emerginglifecoaching.com

Email: janelle@emerginglifecoaching.com

Facebook: https://www.facebook.com/emerginglifecoaching/

Made in the USA
Middletown, DE
18 March 2018